Imani Faith Publishing
Presents

No Test No Testimony In Times Like These
A Look Back at 2020

Compiled by
Cheryl Lacey Donovan

Imani Faith
Publishing
Where faith without works is dead

Legal Notice:

This book is copyright protected. This is only for personal use.

You cannot amend, distribute, sell, use, quote or paraphrase any part of the content within this book without the author's consent. Legal action will be pursued if this is breached.

Disclaimer Notice:

Please note the information contained within this document is for educational and entertainment purposes only. Every attempt has been made to provide accurate, up to date reliable, and complete information. No warranties of any kind are expressed or implied.

.

By reading this document, the reader agrees that under no circumstances are we responsible for any losses, direct or indirect, which are incurred because of the use of the information contained within this document, including, but not limited to, errors, omissions, or inaccuracies.

Acknowledgments and Dedications

I would first like to thank the prolific authors who agreed to participate in this testimony to God's grace during trying times. Each of them has shared their heart in a way that is intended to inspire and empower others during these trying times.

In compiling this anthology, I was reminded about a song entitled "In Times Like These." In this song, we are reminded that our anchor should be the solid rock that is Jesus. My prayer is that after reading this book, you will be able to anchor yourself to the only sure thing- we all have, our faith

Read and be blessed by the testimonies, thoughts, and reflections of Keith K.L. Belvin, Carla Victoria Wallace, Kathy Maqsood, Letisha

No Test No Testimony in Times Like These

Galloway, MarQes Diallo, Lekya Slaughter, and
Cheryl Lacey Donovan.

Table of Contents

2020 According to K.L.
Keith K.L. Belvin — 01

Walking History Book
Carla Victoria Wallace — 16

The World Calls It Quarantine
Kathy Maqsood — 23

A Year of Uncertainty
Letisha Galloway — 29

MarQes' 2020 Testimony
MarQues Diallo — 50

An Experience that Was Sent
Lekya Slaughter — 59

Staying Calm and Centered in Times of Corona Panic
Cheryl Lacey Donovan — 82

A Prayerful Response to the Coronavirus
Cheryl Lacey Donovan — 89

2020 According to K.L.

Keith K.L. Belvin

2020 will go down as one of those years where everyone in the world will look back to reflect on the emotions invoked as the pandemic spread from one country to another. The current crisis is one of those life-altering situations that you can never forget. The sad part is right now, as I write this, we do not know when the world's problems connected to COVID-19 will end. Yes, I said COVID-19 because it is how everybody will remember 2020. I am no different.

Let me give you a little bit about me and how this scourge has changed my life. I am Keith K. L. Belvin, happily married and father of seven. You will have to read my book "From Gigolo to Jesus" to understand the history behind my family configuration. Currently, I am a crisis specialist who works with struggling families. I also counsel singles and couples, which allows me to meet many different types of people. I am also an author. I was an educator and dean of students with the New York City Dept of Education for over 20 years before moving to Delaware to continue saving lives. I own two businesses, a consultant company, Bravin Consultants LLC, and a publishing company, Bravin Publishing LLC. The Bravin name as derived from the first three letters of my wife's maiden name and the last three of mine.

Over the years, I have used my business platform to help as many people as I can move their lives to a higher height. The level of fear and worry is high for a man of color so, I share with you who I am to bring your attention to the idea that there are multiple roads to travel during a pandemic. I hope to bring light to how you can still advance and prosper during such dark times.

"Keep this Book of the Law always on your lips; meditate on it day and night, so that you may be careful to do everything written in it. Then you will be prosperous and successful. 9 Have I not commanded you? Be strong and courageous. Do not be afraid; do not be discouraged, for the Lord, your God will be with you wherever you go." Joshua 1:8-9

In 2020, the level of pain experienced put all of us to the test. The gravest of all the problems we have faced centers around avoiding the virus while still maintaining some routine in our lives. This current plague has opened my eyes to the issues that happen when death is in the air. I do not get fearful due to my faith and belief that the Lord will cover me through this.

"So do not fear, for I am with you; do not be dismayed, for I am your God. I will strengthen you and help you; I will uphold you with my righteous right hand." Isaiah 41:10

Let's break this down. First, there were over forty people, forty-two to be exact, who died from the COVID-19 virus in and around my life. One of those individuals was my mother, who passed on June 25th, 2020, from a massive coronary. She did not have any heart problems, she had other ailments, but not heart problems. When you start to put the numbers together and analyze everything going on, you'll realize what happened. Each of the forty-two people who died had a special story in my life. To think such a large amount of people, since the middle of March, are no longer here gives you a glimpse of the devastation around me and so many others in the world, which is challenging. However, I stood firm during this time, and I did not let fear crush me.

As a crisis specialist, I call upon people to bring their pain to me, so I must find different ways to help others. I invoke others to search me out with their problems because, in doing so, it allows me to unleash my God's gift of intense empathy for other people's problems.

Many do not want to stand in the shoes of others who are in pain due to the weight it places on their shoulders. There are not many people in the world who will say to someone, together we can search through this mud to find the lotus flowers in your life.

COVID-19 has put every part of the abilities that I have to the test. First, it attacked the people around me, forced me to step in, and try to be everything I could. It grew closer and started to pick off coworkers and people I have known and hung out with.

Finally, COVID crept into my family, and I believe it claimed my mother. I share all of this with you to let you know just how devastating COVID has been. Nevertheless, it did not break me. It did not reduce my fight or my will to create. It caused me to reassess myself and forced me to fight to become somebody new.

We wake up every day and try to be who God created us to be. At least we try. But when there is an opposing force pressing upon you, nipping at you with death on its lips, well, your fight or flight response begins to kick in. But what happens when you cannot run? What happens when you cannot go out and hangout? You cannot go out to get air, and if you do, you must make sure you are covered up, so nothing gets into your mouth or nose. What do you do?

Well, for me, I made the decision, if I was going to quarantine myself by remaining close to home, I was going to better myself. If I were not going to do what I enjoy doing, like going to the park with my daughter, tournament bowling, and just being amongst people, I would have to find an alternative outlet to keep me sane. I had to figure out something else to do. So, I decided to work on myself. I asked myself, "what skills can I add, and what area of business can I tackle in these dark times?"

The answer? I started my second business. Yes. Amid this pandemic, I decided to make my counseling business official and made it an LLC in Delaware. As of July, I was already helping people. I was already offering consultations. I was already doing my best to be there for people, but it was time to step up and do more. I wanted to officially stamp my flag in the ground and say to COVID-19, you will not stop me. If I limit any opportunity for this virus to get close to me while still trying to help other people, I am winning, or at least that is how I feel. I do not hold direct sessions anymore due to the virus. I do it virtually to remain safe and not place anyone I am working with in jeopardy.

Because of this leap of faith in a trying time, I have been able to extend my business by opening myself to family, singles, couples, and many others in crisis struggling to make it.

I am determined not to allow COVID-19 to claim any more from me than it already has. Now the virus is going to do what it does, and we are currently riding it out. However, whoever is reading this, knows the current death toll is over 230,000. I do not know what the total will be when you read this book, but I pray they have found a vaccine and that things are starting to return to normal.

Daily I get on this computer, and I try to lift people's spirits. I am a child of God. And that leads me to part two. Another thing I started to do during this COVID-19 pandemic was to get closer to the Lord? At the beginning of my story, I did not say this, but I am an ordained minister through Universal Life Church. I do not wave my Bible and run around trying to gain people's attention, saying, Hey, look at me; I am a minister. No, that is not what I do. I became an ordained minister because I did not want to beg anybody's church to see or help me serve and teach about the Lord. Faith is what I lean on through all of this; trusting God is what I believe in to help me grow. I do not beat people over the head with my faith. I use my confidence; God will make a way as an example of how to remain whole.

When other people say, Hey, K. L., how do you stay vibrant in all this? How do you stay so focused? How do you stay so calm? I'll say it's because of God, and my belief in Jesus Christ as my Lord and Savior. That is what keeps me sane.

"Trust in the Lord with all your heart and lean not on your own understanding; in all your ways submit to him, and he will make your paths straight." **Proverbs 3:5-6**

My spiritual side connection allows me to ask people to bring me their pain as a Crisis Specialist. During this time of COVID-19, devotional faith is the foundation of everything I do. I read the Bible and use it as a primary source when counseling and consulting others. Hence it drives me to offer as much help as I can to other people. I was rewarded in my business due to the faith's acceptance in a time of need and fear.

In getting closer to the Lord, I started some social media groups and made myself available online to other people who are not as strong as I am. I have learned many may be struggling, so by setting up locations online, I can reach out daily and help them.

Finally, I want to share this. No man or woman knows what is coming tomorrow. If you are reading this story, I want you to take the time and ask yourself, in what areas of your life do you need help? How can one help you with changing towards the positive? What are the things you could be doing despite what is happening around you now with COVID-19 or anything else?

I do not know where in the world you may be when you read this, but I pray my words touch your soul and motivate you to push harder in these. I know we are limited in the things we can do without taking the risk of exposure. However, regardless of the current storm, ask yourself, "will I let this virus take more away from me than it already has?"

I challenge you with these questions because we often look at what is lost, not what is gained. Many of us do not look at what is available to us. We don't ask ourselves how we can immerse ourselves into a new life, even with death all around.

"The Lord is my shepherd; I lack nothing. He makes me lie down in green pastures, he leads me beside quiet waters, he refreshes my soul. He guides me along the right paths for his name's sake. Even though I walk through the darkest valley, I will fear no evil, for you are with me; your rod and your staff, they comfort me. You prepare a table before me in the

presence of my enemies. You anoint my head with oil; my cup overflows. Surely your goodness and love will follow me all the days of my life, and I will dwell in the house of the Lord forever." Psalm 23

Many do not believe that if they change their mindset during a pandemic, they can come out on the other side clean. But you can. With all that COVID-19 is trying to destroy, you can still excel and grow into something extraordinary. I am living proof. I followed this line of thinking to help place me on a growth path in my family and business ventures. Recently, I signed up and got a business coach; shout out to Glen P Brooks, Jr. I needed someone who would give me instruction in some areas where I felt I needed assistance to reach a new level. Taking on a coach has allowed me to start targeting my areas of struggle business-wise.

I bring all this to your attention in this story because I want you to understand this about me;

when something comes at me and looks to destroy me, there are only two choices to be made; fold up and allow it to kill me or stand firm and push back with everything I have. I choose the latter and pray that after reading this, you will too.

I wake up every day, and I put a positive message on social media. I start on Instagram, and then onto Facebook, Monday through Friday. In every message, I say, "I do not know who this is for." The reason I make this statement is because I never know where my words will land. I know if I put a positive affirmation out to the world, it may change someone's life.

I don't know who may read this or how their life will be touched. I don't know when you will read this, but when you do, wherever you are, whoever you are, I want you to understand you're stronger than your current position. Even if you feel you are in a position of strength, you can still reach another level. We are all dealing with this COVID-19 crisis, and if you have lost someone to COVID-19, I do not want you to have fears. I want you to be smart. I want you to be healthy. I want you to understand the power inside you. If you are brave enough to unleash it, your life will change forever. You will see clarity, and you will see an opening, and you will see all that is going on around you because God has given the power.

Thank you for taking the time to read. If we never get a chance to meet you, know these words are the words of a COVID-19 survivor. No, I was never infected with COVID-19 myself. I am not trying to get close to it. When I say COVID-19 survivor, it is because I refuse to allow what COVID-19 has tried to destroy around me to stop me from moving forward. In these paragraphs I have shared my heart and what I have learned. I pray that this helps, I do not know who this is for, but I pray it moves you to do more. Take care.

God bless.

Keith K. L. Belvin, MHSC, MS Ed.

Walking History Book

Carla Victoria Wallace

I've been called a walking history book

You may not know my story at first look

The great great-granddaughter of a slave

First one off the boat

On a plantation in South Carolina

Restricted from the right to vote

Granddaughter of sharecroppers

In a North Carolina Town

Through hard work and a dream

They refused to be held down

To the North, they traveled

Were able to buy a house

As a hairstylist and a mason made a better life than they had in the South

Daughter of the first college graduate in her family

No Test No Testimony in Times Like These

My mother set a great example

For those who followed her to see

My father showed great courage

The first to integrate schools in his town

A U.S. Navy veteran

For that, he's made me proud

I followed my mother's footsteps

Graduated with two degrees

Became an elementary school teacher

A writer of books and poetry

I became the wife of a Jamaican

A product of his parent's success

They sent their kids to college

Encouraged them to do their best

I am the mother of three daughters

Who all work hard in school

I train them to follow God

I teach them that learning is cool

Their school shows Dr. King's dream

No Test No Testimony in Times Like These

It has students of every color

Different races and backgrounds

Learning from each other

Daughter of the first college graduate in her family

Different races and backgrounds

Are learning with each other

Have you learned about your family's history?

The people who paved the way

The sacrifices that were made

What shaped who you are today?

Whatever your story maybe

I encourage you to tell it boldly

So that others can truly appreciate their right to be
free

© 2020 Carla Victoria Wallace

When I wrote this poem in January of 2020, I could not explain exactly what came over me, but I felt like the words coming into my mind had to be put to paper immediately. After I put the words to paper, I felt like I had to do something I had never done before; I felt I had to share the words, in public, in front of people. I had attended the Annual Spoken Word/Poetry Tribute held at the Holiday Inn located in Bridgeport, CT, in the past and participated. Still my participation had been as an author vendor, never as a spoken word artist. However, I was obedient to the nudging in my spirit, and I chose to share this poem on February 29th, 2020, at the 11th Annual Spoken Word/Poetry Tribute. I am shy by nature, so this was a huge leap of faith for me.

However, the poem was more well- received than I could have imagined. The result was a mix of attendees standing and shedding tears as they thought of their own personal stories and family history. After the event I was approached by one of the participants. They shared with me how they had overcome their own difficulties. It was my poem that had inspired them to share. I feel like that's what we as writers have the potential to do; we can encourage and inspire with our words.

After sharing this poem, little did I know that by March, a pandemic would shut down the United States socially and economically. We could no longer socialize at large events like the one I had just attended to share this poem, nor could I teach in a classroom full of students indefinitely.

Then, out of nowhere, a horrific incident of police brutality would be caught on video in May 2020, leading to protests against police brutality and the initiation of anti-racism movements. African Americans across the nation began sharing their painful experiences of racism in America, from slavery to segregation to present-day effects of systemic racism past or present.

Recently I attended a professional development training on equity for my job. I was the only person of color in my group. When given the opportunity to share my experiences with racism, I was asked if it made me uncomfortable to share with the group. My response was that I felt it to be freeing to openly speak about something that I always knew still existed. I am encouraged by the newfound willingness of others to listen to the encounters of those who have experienced racism. I hope that it can lead to more progress in our society.

Despite the sad events that we witnessed in 2020, I would like to encourage us to know that we can overcome through faith, hard work, and perseverance. If you feel led to advocate for change in your community, we can do so peacefully. Especially when doing so for those who may not know how to advocate for themselves

On a personal level, we can use the extra time from social distancing to research how to start the business that we may have always wanted to start or write the literary work we always wanted to write or learn a new skill that can open the door to a new career which can impact our communities for the better. Let us learn from our ancestors who overcame that we too can overcome if we do not give up.

I pray that the words in this chapter give us an idea of how we can all look back on 2020 and discover that we have become our own encouraging Walking History   Book.

The World Calls It Quarantine

Kathy Maqsood

2020 has been a year of many trials accompanied by much loss, pain, and suffering. We faced seemingly insurmountable situations as individuals, families, communities, cities, and nations. We have been stretched by the insecurities and fears that we face. Dreams and plans have been sifted through our fingers so many times leaving the future filled with uncertainties and disappointments or new visions and realignments in life. Hope has been deferred repeatedly in so many lives, and as a nation, the heart is sick. The loss of loved ones passing without those dearest to their hearts nearby has left empty places where goodbyes were left unsaid. These are moments that cannot be regained. The trauma of the nation through fires and weather systems seems as if we all have been dreaming. Without warning, hundreds of thousands of folks were displaced through situations in which we had no control. Our belief systems have been challenged as Christians and as a nation. It is a very sobering time. The deepest depths of pain and unresolved issues have surfaced and are being expressed in many ways.

The brutal entrance of Covid-19 into our nation pressured our leaders to make many tough decisions, one of which was lockdown and isolation. Individuals who tested positive were isolated from others to prevent the spread of the virus, while others were placed in quarantine if uncertain exposure to the virus was suspected. I was pondering all these things one day when Holy Spirit spoke a word to my heart. He said the world calls it isolation, but I call it SEPARATION.

Families and friends were no longer permitted

to connect at favorite gathering places but asked to reside within their homes. As God's children there is nothing that is permitted to touch our lives of which He is unaware. It is during times when we seem to have no control that God will do the deepest work in our hearts and lives.

Too many times, our "homes" had become "houses." A home is where love is abounding. Fellowship is found within the walls and the lives of those within are full of affection. The home is to be a safe, restful, peaceful dwelling place. Our culture has produced so many convenient excuses for us to retreat to a separate room or activity instead of having personal interaction in the home. Much pressure was produced in the many areas of unresolved offenses festering within the family. Emotions from embittered hearts have begun surfacing all over the nation.

Our precious Redeemer, the Lord Jesus Christ,

is redeeming this time to regather what has been scattered-our relationship with Him and among family members, friends, and groups of people. The spirit of the world has invaded. And God is a jealous God. He is regathering his family. We may have asked Him to come into our hearts but never built a relationship with Him. Or we may have walked in intimacy in a past season, but life simply got in the way, and our hearts strayed. Nothing can separate us from His love. However hidden sin in the heart or distractions can prevent us from connecting with His presence, which is what the core of the family is all about. We have placed expectations upon others to fill this void that no person nor material thing can satisfy. It is in the home where love is to be mirrored. It is a gathering place to learn about God, His kingdom, training in acceptable behavior, a place of unity with peace, and extending mercy and grace to one another. Home is to be a place of respect.

We are called to the ministry of reconciliation. What has been reconciled in your life, family, or relationships during this year? God wants our personal borders and boundaries in place and secured. We must use our authority that He has given us in the name of Jesus and call forth order out of chaotic areas of our lives. We need our own personal vision and not someone else's. There is grace for the specific calling upon our lives and if I am trying to build in an area to which I am not called, I will be miserable. Getting out of my lane results in constant turmoil with jealousy, envy, and strivings within.

God is cleaning His house. We are His temple. Many folks spent the first months cleaning and bringing back order where life had displaced priorities. We must flourish as His body so His glory can flow through us into the world. From the mother's womb, each of us was separated for the work of the ministry to which we are called. Is this season all about ME or YOU, or is about realigning our hearts and life to prepare us so that our destiny with the Lord can be fulfilled? Are you separated for regathering in your life and taking back what has been robbed, or has self, life and the enemy continued to scatter? The sword of the Lord is going through families. Am I in the role of someone else? Do I need to prefer others before myself? This will require dying to all the fleshy behaviors and attitudes that we have entertained. As we approach 2021, what fruit will be manifested from this season of our lives? Will it be the kingdom of God or the kingdom of self? Do you know who you are now? So many things have been cut away or pruned. So, what remains in your life from this season of being separated?

A Year of Uncertainty

Letisha Galloway

The New Year is a time for reflection and hope. The year 2020 was of significance to me because I graduated high school 20 years ago. I, like many others was looking forward to this year being a great year. Because our class reunion was approaching. I wanted to see those who I had not seen since our teenage years. It would have been interesting to see how all our lives turned out. Perhaps in 2021, I will be able to catch up with my friends, those who I have always been friends with, and those who I became friends with after we left high school.

At the end of 2019, I declared that 2020 was going to be my year. Little did I know that the pandemic would "steal my shine." I decided to push some projects back to the end of 2020 and the beginning of 2021. Some required me to be around people, and it was just not safe to be around many people at the time. I was very disappointed so, my situational depression continued throughout the year.

The year 2020 started out with tragedy. In January, the shocking news came that sports icon Kobe Bryant, his daughter and seven others perished in a helicopter crash. As they showed the wreckage on television, it seemed unreal. Kobe and the Los Angeles Lakers were a big part of basketball. He is, and will remain, one of my generation's great icons. When Kobe died, it was the first time I've seen some men cry. Although many of us didn't know Kobe, he did arrive in our living rooms via televisions often.

While Kobe was being mourned, the news of COVID-19 was moved to the back burner. Although we were warned of an impending outbreak in November, no one, including the President, seemed to take it seriously. I must admit I didn't take it as seriously as I should have. It wasn't until things shut down in March that I began to take a second look. I thought it was a disease that would stay overseas. I, like many others, was not ready for the mass hysteria.

Some people are still not taking it seriously. Some are walking around without masks, don't wash their hands or sanitize. Not only do they put themselves at risk of getting COVID 19, but they may also be exposing others to it, which is selfish. Those who did take the pandemic seriously found themselves unable to find hand sanitizer at a reasonable price for months. I saw hand sanitizer being sold for $30 and thought, UNBELIEVABLE!

COVID-19 hit close to home when two of my friend's children had it, two of my cousins had it, two associates had it, and my former boss died from it. When I found out my former boss died from it, I was in total shock. His death made it real. The thought that someone could retire and enjoy their life one minute and then be gone because of COVID the next was heartbreaking to say the least. Some former coworkers (active and retired) were devastated. A few had to go home for the day. Just like Kobe's family, friends, and fans, my former boss's family, friends, and former coworkers now needed time to grieve too. Grief takes on many forms and while some were grieving the loss of a loved one, others were grieving the loss of special moments that should have been etched in their memories for a lifetime.

The class of 2020 faced a lot of uncertainty. Would they be able to attend graduation? What about their prom? Well, the answer to that is, the class was not permitted to have prom in person. Some schools had virtual proms, which is not by far the same experience even though it was a nice try.

I remember prom as a time of socialization and fashion. Unfortunately, I had on the same dress as a few of my friends. Nonetheless, I had a great time.

The Class of 2020 was robbed of their prom and Found themselves grieving the fun time they would have had. They mourned the pictures that would never be taken and the dances that would never be danced in those special moments.

As if the Class of 2020 was not hit hard enough, they missed out on graduation as well. High school and college students missed out on graduation. Yes, many had a virtual experience where they showed your picture, but that is by far not the same experience as walking across the stage to everyone clapping. Even though loved ones tried their best to recreate the moment, prom and graduation was not the same for the class of 2020.

To add insult to injury, minorities risked having their lives stolen based on the color of their skin! With the recent deaths of George Floyd and Breonna Taylor, tensions between minorities and the police were tenser than ever. The mistrust on both sides was tangible.

George Floyd was arrested on May 25, 2020. The police were called because a store clerk believed Floyd used fake money to buy cigarettes. Floyd was pinned beneath an officer's knee and became unconscious after more than 8 minutes. The officer did not remove his knee off Floyd's neck even after Mr. Floyd became unconscious. With the video footage and witnesses, murder charges were brought against the officer. There has been a debate about the amount of time the knee was on Mr. Floyd's neck. But, does it really matter whether it was 7 or 8 minutes? I don't believe it does. The man became unconscious and died in police custody after he begged for his life, and others tried to help.

The killing didn't stop at George Floyd: it continued with Breonna Taylor. It was reported that the police did not announce themselves after banging on the door. It was in the early morning hours that the officers tried to enter Breonna's apartment. Neighbors reported that they did not hear a police announcement, even though the police were adamant it was announced. Breonna's boyfriend fired warning shots because he believed someone was attempting to break into the apartment. One of the bullets struck an officer after the warning shot was fired. In response, the officers blindly unloaded 32 bullets into the apartment. Some of the bullets entered a neighboring apartment. There could have been collateral damage. Breonna was hit with five or six bullets and within minutes she lay dead in her apartment.

The deaths of George Floyd and Breonna Taylor could have been avoided. They are two of many lives lost because of police brutality against minorities. George Floyd's death could have been prevented if the officers had listened to him when he said he couldn't breathe. Floyd called out for his deceased mother before finally relenting to the inevitable, death. That is tragic. There was no need to have an officer restrict Floyd's airways for 7 or 8 minutes (depending on what news media is followed). The murder was caught on video. If there wasn't any video footage, I believe the officers would have gotten away with murder.

The death of Breonna Taylor could have been prevented by not blindly firing 32 shots into the apartment. It shows that the police entered, not caring who they shot. The person who fired the shots is still alive, while Taylor died in her own apartment. That night will forever be etched in some of our minds as senseless. The police could have killed the neighbors too. Blindly shooting doesn't seem like it would be included in police training.

It is because of deaths like George Floyd and Breonna Taylor that the Black Lives Matter Movement was formed. The movement isn't to say all lives don't matter because they do but, we want others to recognize that Black Lives Matter too. Minorities are being killed by police at an alarming rate so, it stands to reason that there needs to be widespread police sensitivity training because many of these situations are unwarranted. I fear for the many minorities (especially men) who face a world that is afraid of them.

My three nephews are smaller now: 11, 9, and 4 years old, respectively. I still worry about them. I especially worry about the 11-year-old because he is close to the age of 12-year-old Tamir Rice, who was shot a few years ago while playing with a fake gun in the park. The police did not ask any questions; they just shot him. They did not take the time to see if it was a child or that the gun was fake. It depresses me to think that it is not safe for my nephew to walk around and mind his own business. We live in a sad world where a child cannot walk down the street or enter a store without being followed around like a common criminal because of the color of their skin.

It is my hope that what Civil Rights Leader John Lewis has done throughout the years will not be in vain. I believe the Black Lives Matter Movement has taken up where he left off. He died in 2020 at the age of 80 years old. He was a front runner in the civil rights movement who organized many marches, such as the Selma to Montgomery march over 50 years ago. He believed in non-violence like that exhibited by the Black Lives Matter Movement. The media would have people believe that the movement is violent because of the rioting and looting that took place in 2020 but these people were not a part of the Black Lives Matter Movement. A lot of people came from out of town to destroy and loot. There were white people caught defacing property and looting. On video, Black Lives Matter protesters can be heard asking people to stop.

Close to 200 black lives were lost due to police brutality and systematic murder in 2020. We honor them. Their lives were not in vain. There will be change. The question is, how many more people must die for there to be widespread police reform? I don't have the answer but what I do know is that this must stop. The way whites are treated is different than blacks. Anytime a mass shooter like Dylan Roof can get a burger while waiting to be escorted, and a minority gets 32 bullets, there is something wrong with that. It must be fixed.

The year 2020 brought economic uncertainty. Many people lost their jobs because of the pandemic. As a case manager, I process benefits for food, medical insurance, childcare, and cash assistance. I have seen countless people laid off from all kinds of industries. I've seen everyone from a restaurant worker to a hairstylist laid off or closed for business. Some small businesses did not survive the economic crisis.

Every month we receive hundreds of

applications from people who are being negatively affected by the pandemic economically. There are some we can help within the guidelines and others we cannot. Going through this pandemic has made me appreciate my job. Yes, my job stresses me, and yes, I will seek other employment in the future, but for the time being, my job is secure, and I am grateful. One of the stories could have been mine, but I thank God that it is not my story. I pray for the families and people that are affected by this pandemic financially.

One of the things that I like that Social Services is doing is that they cannot close a person's medical coverage during the pandemic. Many people who would be disqualified by new or returning income will stay open in Medicaid. These families could not afford health care. Consequently, I feel bad for the new applications that must be denied because of income. Some miss the mark by only a few dollars of being over the income. Who gets Medicaid, and who doesn't is a chapter by itself? I will move on.

The year 2020 brought about the loss of one of my truest friends. This was non- Covid 19 related, but it stung, nonetheless. When I found out, I was completely devastated. I didn't know what to think or do. I simply felt stunned. We messaged regularly, even if it was a quick joke or to check on one another. I didn't know how I was going to process the grief. We had plans to meet up in the summer of 2021 after I finished visiting with family. I was looking forward to it. Now all I must look forward to is visiting his grave if I can bring myself to do it.

After he died, I started to slip into a depression. There were things that happened good that I wanted to share with him, and I couldn't anymore, and it tore me apart. I had to remember he wasn't here anymore. It took some getting used to not hearing from him. It still feels strange to talk about him in the past tense. It's going to take time. The grieving process doesn't take a day. It was important for me to remember that I lost a true friend and it's ok to cry.

The year 2020 has brought about an increase in depression. Prior to the pandemic, 8.5% of adults in the United States reported experiencing depression. The 8.5% has increased to 27.8% as the pandemic continues (Berman,2020). It has doubled. Common stressors include the death of a loved one, financial obligations/debt, and the fear of losing it all. Millions of people in the United States have lost their jobs due to the pandemic. The number continues to rise as small businesses close. "Individuals with less than $5,000 in savings were 50% more likely to be experiencing symptoms of depression than those who had more (Berman,2000). While finances contribute to the rise in depression, it is not the only culprit.

The isolation is very real. For most, we were told to stay away from our loved ones. We were told not to interact with people for fear of infection. We have been banned from social events, attending church and any activity that requires close interaction. Those that are depressed need social interaction to keep from being isolated. Isolation allows time for negative thoughts and feelings of loneliness to enter. When loneliness enters, the suicide rate increases, depression increases, and anxiety increases as well.

The depression and suicide are affecting health care workers as well. Dr. Lorna Breen, an emergency room doctor in New York City, took her life. She was working 18-hour days. She contracted Covid-19 and was sent home to recuperate. (Kelly, 2020). Her family reported her as disturbed and detached because of her seeing an alarming rate of death from Covid-19 at the hospital she worked in. The pandemic is affecting everyone. It doesn't matter what social or economic class that you're in.

The Center for Disease Control conducted a

survey of 5,412 people between June 24 and June 30th. The data collected was astonishing, to say the least. "Roughly 25% of young adults between the ages of 18 to 24 years of age said they considered suicide because of the pandemic. Thirty-one percent of the respondents reported they had symptoms of anxiety and depression. Twenty-six percent of those surveyed reported trauma and stress-related disorders related to the pandemic. Close to 14 % of those surveyed said that they used alcohol, prescription/illegal drugs to cope with the pandemic. (Kelly, 2020).

The statistics are not startling to me. As a person who has dealt with mental illness and isolation during a depressive episode, I understand what isolation can do. I was a young adult who experienced isolation even if it was self-imposed at times (after my son died, I didn't feel like talking). Isolation causes the mind to have time for a flood of negative thoughts. When a person is isolated, there is no one to tell them that there is a better day coming. There is no one to cry to or listen. There is always God, but I am speaking in the natural. When I experienced depression, God was the last person on my mind because I had convinced myself that I am unlovable.

During this pandemic, I've learned that there are people who are experiencing depression in this difficult time just like I am. Grant it, it's not isolation anymore, but it saddens me to turn on the news. The people dying from the pandemic has saddened me. I've cried out. In New York City, as the bodies piled up, I questioned why this was happening. I said there must be something that I am supposed to learn from this. So, here it is. From the pandemic, I learned that life is too precious to spend on meaningless drama, arguments or being unhappy. Instead, life should be more about telling people you love them every day. We don't know when COVID-19 will go away or even if it will go away. What I know is that people I know have suffered through it. Every precaution that can be made should be made. Change is upon us.

On November 7, 2020, President Donald Trump lost his reelection. The country had been divided through most of his presidency. It may have taken a few more days than we would have liked but Joe Biden being elected President is the best thing for our country right now. There needs to be a leader who will bring this pandemic under control in the best way possible. In my opinion, President-elect Joe Biden will help pass some of the best policies for the poor and working class. The higher taxes were meant for those making $400,000 or more per year. I'm not worried about it. Biden received a record number of votes that surpassed even that of President Barack Obama. That's history-making.

Vice President-elect Kamala Harris has made history. She has made history as not only a woman but a black woman. Black little girls are going to see themselves in a great position of power in Kamala Harris. That's powerful. Little girls who have never seen themselves in the president or vice president history books will now have a chance to. There will be media coverage on Kamala Harris and I, as a black woman, plan on buying whatever I can that represents her. I plan on talking about Kamala Harris with my nieces and I plan on sharing the importance of the moment, the moment a black woman took a high office in our country; what it means for now and the future. I plan to share with them that if Kamala Harris can do great things, they can too.

I am looking forward to a better 2021. Prayerfully the year will start off in a positive way. I want to see my family and friends happy and healthy. I pray that Covid goes away, never to return. It's a vicious disease that has taken way too many lives.

In 2021 I pray that things for students get back

to some sense of normalcy. It will be a great time when my nieces, nephews and other children will be able to return to school. Children need that social interaction and instruction you just cannot get from a zoom meeting. I pray the teenagers get to experience prom and graduation in person. These times cannot be replaced. I pray that the graduates get to walk across the stage in 2021 and accept that diploma or degree they worked so hard for. I pray that the injustices against minorities be brought to light so that there can be a resolution. I pray that the depression and burdens be lifted off people in this season. They need to know that someone cares.

I'm praying that all of my friends are healthy and that I do not lose any of them in 2021, as I am still grieving the loss of a dear friend, I lost in 2020. It is my hope in 2021 that more people come to know Jesus Christ. It is my hope that many come to realize that they are loveable, but first, they must love themselves.

I pray that 2021 is a better year for me. I plan on launching some things in 2021 that did not happen in 2020. The main thing that we can do is pray and then try to prepare for what 2021 has in store. I hope to launch out the projects I have in mind. Stay tuned. May you have a blessed and prosperous 2021.

References

Berman, R. (2020, September 19). *US cases of depression have tripled during the COVID-19 pandemic.*

Medical News Today.
https://medicalnewstoday.com/articles

Kelly, J. (2020, August 18). *The pandemic has caused an increase in anxiety, stress, depression and suicides.* Getty.
https://www.forbes.com/sites/jackkelly

MarQes' 2020 Testimony

MarQes Diallo

Hello, I wanted to introduce myself. My name is MarQes, and I am 12 years old and the CEO of The MarQes Enterprises. I am a motivational speaker, I sell inspirational items, and I have recently started working more on my technical skills with a business called The MarQes Studios. With MarQes Studios I work on filming, podcasting, and creating websites. I am sharing my testimony of the pandemic and all the things that took place beginning March 2020 in hopes that it will encourage someone to move passed the darkness and into the light.

The pandemic was very overwhelming, stressful, and discouraging. I can remember when my teacher talked with my class: he mentioned that the pandemic was bad. It was a possibility that the schools would be closed, and we would no longer be able to see one another daily. On that same day, we had to take everything out of our lockers in preparation for the shutdown. It was all on the news. At first, I was excited after all, it was a break from school, but that feeling soon ended as the days turned into weeks and the weeks into months. However, because I was accepted into a program that was well known for entrepreneurs called Allstate Minority and Women Emerging Entrepreneurs program (2020-2021) my angst turned into gratefulness because I would start in the fall.

Who knew that shortly after, not only school would be closing, but churches, grocery stores, doctor's offices, and more? Remote learning and trying to meet deadlines were tough. It affected my grades tremendously because although I work very hard with my education, it was difficult. After all I would often stay up late completing and submitting work online. Sometimes, because of glitches in technology, my grades would not be reflected. It was a lot to deal with. I experienced headaches, discouragement, and sometimes I just felt down because the world appeared to be crashing around us. I was not able to focus on much of anything, including my business.

My normal activities were disrupted. I noticed my focus was different; my communication with my mom was different. I would often shut down, even though she would respond differently each time, by asking, is there anything I can do to help you? When you are ready to talk, I am here? How can I help you? Eventually, she began to get frustrated, and we would often have meetings about my behavior and attitude. Although, she allowed me space and time to share what I was feeling, I often would end up on punishment. Many times, I did not know how to express how I was feeling and did not want to be disrespectful. I knew I had to come up with a solution and change my ways because my behavior was not helping me.

The death of many prominent people and the racism and killings that took place during this time was very difficult for the world. It was in the media daily. I know I had family around me to support however, the daily barrage of negative information affected me emotionally and mentally. It all became very stressful and overwhelming. One of the biggest disappointments came when I was nominated to attend the Harvard Ambassador Leadership Program Summer 2020. Due to the pandemic, it was canceled and would not resume until 2021. Fundraising ceased, vending that I often did had ceased and many of the extracurricular activities I participated in ceased. My world was turned upside down.

Church, my mentoring program, soccer, even my Doctor's appointments were all being done virtually now. It felt weird. There was no outlet. The media kept us up to date with what was going on. It was sad seeing how many families were being impacted around the world.

Seeing the brutality that unfolded in 2020 was also shocking. I often wondered what Dr. Martin Luther King Jr. would have done or thought with the realities that we, as a race of people, are still facing. According to Dr. Martin Luther King Jr, "Darkness cannot drive out darkness; only light can do that. Hate cannot drive out hate; only love can do that."

Summer was different. School had ended, and I was able to briefly participate in another program. Once the program ended, I was able to get rest and have more peace of mind. During the program, I received guidance and help with my business. The feedback was great. I received some coaching sessions regarding my passion for doing websites as a service. Getting clarity with some of the products for my apparel line and, my message delivery which helped me with my desire in encouraging people through film, podcast, and creating websites

I am grateful for God and my family, who has been my biggest support despite how I may have wanted to give up on business and my goals. They have always kept me lifted in prayer, encouraging me, and telling me to stay focused. For me, prayer was necessary. I know I would not have been able to do anything without it.

Films have always been one of my passions, along with photography, podcasts, and technical things. I have often created videos at schools and for individuals. I just want to utilize my gifts to continue to encourage others regardless of what they are going through. I have always liked Mr. Tyler Perry. Watching his plays and movies brought joy and laughter during sad times. I hope to one day be able to do the same.

There have been times when my family has gone through stressful situations. During these times however, positivity was spoken into in my life. Especially when Mother Greene, who recently passed during the pandemic passed away. I remembered how she allowed me to minister at her residence on various occasions. She put flyers on her neighbors' door telling them about me. I was only five, but she recognized something in me, that perhaps I didn't even understand. The opportunities continued over the years and I could see the excitement in her and the senior citizens' faces as they would come down to the conference room to see my young rendition of a message from the Lord. We would be singing, reading scriptures, and praising God. I used my children's bible to speak what God gave me.

One of the stories I often read and spoke about was Joseph. It was truly amazing, and, after the service was over, there would be a table filled with recycled bottles that they brought to support my school tuition expenses for the private Christian school I was attending at the time. The pandemic allowed me to reflect and be reminded of some of my biggest supports and prayer warriors. I have learned to appreciate those who cross my path no matter who they may be.

Fall of 2020. Adversity to gratitude was a new year, 7th grade. We had the option to go hybrid/ virtual or fully remote virtually. My learning style requires me to be in the classroom. Although my mom signed me up for fully virtual, she allowed me to advocate for myself. I went to school twice a week and the other days were virtual. I was glad to be back in school and grateful for social interaction because I had not been involved in my normal activities for quite some time. I must be real with you. It was tough. Technical issues were rampant, trying to meet the deadlines again was difficult so, I felt I did worse than I ever had. But one thing I can tell you is, I didn't quit. With the help of my mom, school counselor, principal, staff, and prayer from my family, I was encouraged.

I had to put things in place. Instead of doing the work all at once, I put a schedule in place to pace myself. I stayed resilient. My Nana kept me invigorated by always calling and doing check-ins about my schoolwork.

Now due to the high numbers of Covid, we are remote again a couple of days from Thanksgiving. But I learned no matter what happens, there are a lot of things that are important to me. For that, I am thankful. I am also often reminded of the inspirational quotes and messages that I give people. I encourage them and take the same words I give them for myself. "Get out of the discouraging place. Do everything God has destined for you to do. Let God Handle It! Dream Big Always! Never Give Up

---

An Experience that was Sent

Lekya Slaughter

The Pandemic of 2020 was an experience

An experience that was sent

Sent to a world whose lives are changed forever

Forever and ever and many of us thought never

Never did we think it could happen.I had a hard time trying
to wrap my mind around all of it

All of it; Covid, the brutality, killings, death, and riots

Riots that began in many households; many were
communication barriers

Barriers for me, although, I enjoyed spending time with my
kings and talking with my family

Family, not being able to see them was tough, although I
spent time with them as much as I would have liked.

Like the distance that allow us to know how much our
family means

Means to cherish every moment God has sent like the birth
of my 2nd great-niece who I couldn't visit. God knows I
wish I could

No Test No Testimony in Times Like These

Could see the ways that the distance allowed me to begin
working on myself

Myself, my personal development; praying and asking God
to lead and guide me

Me, with strategic direction into my destiny.

Destiny, you know what, it may sound unreal, but I often
felt like although I was praying, I was still far from God

God, I didn't know what to pray for, but still followed
determination with a nod

With a nod of determination, I continued to pour into my
sons, worked on time management and self- affirmation

Self-affirmation and speaking life were amazing because it
was often easier to pour into everyone

Everyone else but myself.

God and I knew. Soon family and friends began to
understand what I was going through

Through it all I watched God continue to keep and preserve
my family

Family, protected from hurt, harm, and danger

Danger and chaos were going on all in the world

World mothers and father, boys, and girls

No Test No Testimony in Times Like These

Boys and girls seeing denominations across the nations

Nation's seeking God's face without hesitation

Hesitation pleading the blood of Jesus with tears in our
eyes

Eyes swollen with tears because of the passing away of
loved ones; some due to Covid, illness and some otherwise

Otherwise, seeing strangers on social media losing their
lives day by day due to blood that was shed

Shed to soon, and then the Facebook alerts ding, ding,

another one was dead

Dead spirits and heartbroken for families losing their lives
to suicide, domestic violence, mental illness and so much
more,

Often seeing the homeless requesting or some would say
begging as we would go to the store

Store full of people but I stopped, I stopped and often

prayer is what I offered

Offered it knowing God would heal, cover, and make them
softer

Softer in their minds, soul, and heart

The hearts of Giants losing their lives because of what we
could not end

No Test No Testimony in Times Like These

End? But this was a new start

A start for myself and all of us to see ourselves anew

Anew mentally, spiritually, emotionally physically,
socially; restored, healed and closer to God

God could have wiped us out but to God be the glory, He
spared the rod and allowed us a second chance to get
ourselves right. God truly has shed light

Light in spite of the heartbrokenness, depression,

oppression, God sent, joy, laughter, peace and covering

Covering and healing, much of the suffering

Suffering many children experienced in academics

Academics allowed families to be alert and on the same
page with their children, teachers, professors, counselors
and more

More, remember it was a lot that was sent

Sent through it all we're still walking in our destiny

Truly, the pandemic was an experience

The Covid Virus Pandemic changed my life for
the better, Although I had my ups and downs, I can
say God is a keeper. When I tell you But God, you

better believe it! To God, be the glory! He kept me and he kept my family. I made sure we did not want for anything. We have a roof over our heads and food on the table. We were healthy and our family was restored. Bills that would often be overdue and would normally have been disconnected were paid with the extensions put in place to prevent disconnections, shutoffs, and cancellation. I am healed, and overall grateful for the communication, mending and so much more. Some lessons pushed me to self-reflect in so many ways. Often being there to encourage everyone else, mentally, spiritually, emotionally, and physically, I soon learned the necessity of taking care of myself first.

Let me share my story about where I was when the pandemic first began unraveling. A possible shut down was eminent due to the increase of virus cases all around the world. I was truly trusting God, praying, making sure to get all the necessities I could get, and encouraging others. But in my mind due to hearing what was going on in the media, worry and sometimes fear would set in. I had to learn how to shut the noise out and speak God's word. I often found myself saying, I know what they say, but what does God say? Often I recited the scripture from Proverbs: Trust in the LORD with all your heart, and lean not on your understanding; in all your ways acknowledge Him, and He will make your paths straight.

Although I didn't allow the fear to take over, it did take a toll because I often did not know how to feel: I did not know how things would go in regard to my finances. If schools closed, what was my plan B.

Eventually, the inevitable happened. Notices went out that schools were officially closed until further notice. Eventually, my son started remote learning, and at first, he was excited; however, it was stressful and difficult as a mom that has always advocated on behalf of others, not to know how to be his advocate. Nevertheless, I was reminded of this scripture, "Be anxious for nothing, but in everything, by prayer and petition, with thanksgiving, present your requests to God."_I just want to say thank you, God, for allowing me to be alive for a reason.

I began to think about the story in the bible about Pharaoh Let my people go. Exodus 9:1 "Then the LORD said to Moses, "Go to Pharaoh and say to him, This, is what the LORD, the God of the Hebrews, says: Let my people go, so that they may worship me." I often was reminded of how out of all the devastation we were going through, God covered me and my family under the blood.

Worry, mental headaches, sleeping patterns that were off, all of it manifested itself in the wake of the ensuing circumstances. Frustrations were rampant and I often had to check myself. Although I worried at times, God shifted me into praise where I found myself thanking him despite the circumstances. Worship, prayer and fasting were necessary in this time. Doing things afraid became the norm. For instance, I had begun getting into uncomfortable places going live on Facebook. I was just beginning to show up, which wasn't comfortable for me. It was easier for me to assist in the background. However, I began feeling a pull to stop trying to figure it all out. Sometimes it meant allowing God to speak however he desired and getting outside of myself. I had to get out of my way and God's way.

My sensitivity to people only intensified as time went on. I found myself often worrying about children that may have been suffering from neglect or abuse due to being at home and the mental issues that many of the families may have been struggling with before or even the more due to the pandemic. It was heartbreaking. The increase of addiction during this time was apparent as we saw more individuals begging for money. I would often ask if I could pray for them, but with the virus infiltrating every area of our lives, I had to keep a distance.

My son and I volunteered serving food and giving away bookbags to those who needed them. Nevertheless, I was always second guessing my decision because of the reports about the virus's constant assault on the lives of others. I was consistently asking God if it was okay. Sometimes because of the overwhelm and stress I felt, I experienced headaches and sleepless nights. Being there for myself felt awkward because despite everything, I was always sensitive and understanding of the crying out of other people. I can recall many times, being in the car or living room crying out and allowing the tears to roll and *asking* God to take the pieces off me so I could truly be impactful. But now it was time for myself; I had to be made whole.

I began my journey in my own home because even though we are in the house, our families may feel that they're not important because our time is spent doing work on the computer or in conversation with co-workers and other colleagues.

Anxiety and depression creeped in, but after speaking with my counselor, I chose to be intentional about getting closer to God. I began seeing my onsets of my anxiety: there were times that I saw the onsets of my depression. The pandemic pushed me to continue to cry out. It pushed me to continue to fast and deal with my health and wellness while also developing myself personally. I participated in a health challenge and became more disciplined about paying attention to my eating habits and exercise. However, after the challenge was over, I went back to those old habits. I'm still a work in progress.

During the pandemic God blessed me to gain more knowledge with my business than I had done in previous years. Because of this investment in myself, I was able to learn a lot from advisors and coaches of personal development. They taught me that my mindset to this pointy had been one more aligned with a hobby as opposed to an actual business. I needed to change that mindset to propel my business forward. Changing my mindset was so much more important than anything else I could have done because it allowed me to see myself the way God sees me. I was setting myself up to be free of the bondage in my mind that kept me in a place of fear and guilt. The mindset transformation has put me on a path step over my past so that I can walk into the purpose that God has for me. I was now taking the same advice that I had poured into others. They often told me of the accomplishments they made because of my inspiration, yet, I had not taken my own advice. I was grateful that God was working for them but couldn't see how He could do the same for me. Imagine how much more impactful-I could be if I allow God to endow in me and make me over.

My desire to be made whole allowed me to take the layers off. I would often tell people to do the mirror talk, but I had to start doing mirror talk (affirmations) for myself. It was amazing. I began the routines of in my life and soon God sent help to make it more intentional.

A young lady by the name of Ciara sent out an invitation for people to join her Facebook affirmations and prayer group. It was truly a blessing and helped me even more. Even as I'm saying it now, I'm getting emotional because, as I began looking in the mirror saying I Lekya am God's child. l Lekya am loved. I Lekya am special. I Lekya am a QUEEN. I am a powerful, nurturing, caring and phenomenal mom, daughter, sister, auntie, teacher, and friend. I Lekya am filled with God's grace and mercy. I Lekya am more than enough. I Lekya am filled with possibility and gratitude. I Lekya am Walking into my Purpose and Destiny. I LEKYA AM FREE, WALKING FREELY AND SPEAKING FREELY. I Lekya am a survivor. I Lekkya am no longer bound to my past. I Lekya am healed. I Lekya will not be hindered. I Lekya am intentional in all I do. I Lekya am getting my laugh back. I Lekya am no longer second-guessing myself. I Lekya have forgiven. I Lekya forgive myself. I Lekya am beautiful. I Lekya am an intercessor. I Lekya am a prayer warrior. I Lekya am precious. I Lekya am God's Child. You are God's child. I now see the importance of the practice. It is important for me to tell Kia she can be whatever she desires and look at it in that mirror

I had to take layers off me. Those things that I've been hearing from childhood that held me in bondage had to go. Those things that I have allowed myself to be buried in had to be released if I was to go forward and do everything that God needs me to do.

Often saying I was in my way, I realized I wasn't in my way, I was in God's way. Restoration within my family and peace within myself was part of the process.

During the pandemic loved ones and family of loved ones and friends died. Grief was real. I learned the language of grief is not always about how one is doing?

Over time before and throughout the pandemic, I began becoming intentional. I have meetings weekly with my business advisors and coaches, sometimes 2 to 3 times a week. I had to put strategies in place to allow myself to stay laser focused. With the expertise of each person, I developed a plan that helped me identify my target audience, my niche, and my ideal client.

No longer will I just do busy work, never getting anything complete, or having a goal or deadline in mind. Although I still help in many of the same areas business-wise, with guidance, I created a niche in which I help communicate with parents. I give them tools and strategies so they can resolve conflict and have meaningful dialogue with their 11- to 19-year-olds. This in turn helps them to have peace of mind and a calm environment. They now talk to each other and not at each other.

This business unfolded for me as I began to dissect communication barriers. I would often ask my oldest King D to tell me how I was as a mom, what was effective and not effective. His answers helped me to better communicate with my younger son King Qes.

During the pandemic. I would often ask in various ways how I could help. My son's response was often limited. I began to hear a tone in his voice that I was not pleased with and was sure to let him know it wasn't ok. As A mom, I felt I followed through with the best communication I knew but it didn't seem to be working. Fortunately, God sent the village to the rescue. My family and my son's school staff filled in the gaps where my communication may have lacked. I really didn't understand why the same strategies that worked for others were now failing me. It was time to tackle it now before things got worse.

We settled on family meetings where we both expressed how we felt. Each of us allowed the other to express both the good and the bad feelings we had about one another's behavior and attitudes. I did understand the frustration and overwhelm of school. Many of the extracurricular activities he participated in were put to an end. I understood it all. However, it was important for me to set the order.

I allowed him to express his thoughts on the best solution. The loss of electronics was his primary response. Eventually, he got back on task, and we continued to follow up with teachers and staff.

The pandemic was not our only concern. The horrific murder of George Floyd created an additional layer of turmoil in our household. Seeing complete strangers' loved ones being murdered in the street was hurtful. I began to worry about possible receiving a phone call about my family members or even myself being stopped by the police. After all it had happened before, and it wasn't a pleasant experience.

I remember one Thursday night on my way to bible study I was stopped by the police. With my hands in the air, the officer asked, "what's wrong? Why are your hands in the air?"

I responded, "my hands are in the air because I want you to see I have nothing in my hand. I am unsure why I am being stopped."

He was yelling, and I asked him why he was yelling. He said, "you almost killed me."

I apologized, telling him I moved over to the side lane to be sure I wasn't in the way after he put the flashers on. I was still unsure why I was stopped. He told me I could put my hands down after returning with my ID. After that, he looked at my son, and his entire demeanor changed. "I am going to let you Go," he said. I was grateful. We still don't have any effective communication going on about police brutality.

Although I loved going to church, I missed it but was grateful for the continued online access. I remember when the church opened, and my son and I went. My God, tears just rolled. I continued to get in God's face at home in my car, crying out, and listening to soaking music. I often found myself praying with other intercessors. That was a blessing.

Bible study was an effective to deal with what we were facing. To really be able to go into the layers of the word was calming. Being a part of the platform was amazing because God knows what we need, and he knows what we need right now. I needed that.

I thank God for continuing to keep my family. I thank God for keeping my mother. I thank God for keeping my brother, my sister, my nieces my nephew's, and my children. I thank God for keeping me in my right mind. I thank God that he's continuing to heal our hearts, our minds, and souls.

Through this season I have learned that it is terribly important to practice self-care. We give give, give, give, give, give, give, and give some more. We're giving all of us and we don't have anything left for ourselves. It's important to pour into others but it is just as important for us to position ourselves to be poured into. It's non-negotiable.

Lessons learned during the Pandemic

1. **Be Still-** sometimes the noise and what we're hearing and seeing can distract us in our daily lives. Sometimes we just need to turn everything off; social media, phones, computers, and television. Everything. Psalm **46:10** "Be still, and know that I am

God; I will be exalted among the nations, I will be exalted in the earth."

2. **It's not what they say but How you respond.** This saying was real for me. The only person I can control is me. I asked God to help me muzzle my mouth. Staying silent allowed me to develop peace of mind. I noticed my growth. When I was a child, I responded out of anger and aggression. I dealt with people the way they dealt with me. I had to check myself often.

3. **It's not what they say, but what God says!**

4. **It is important to be sensitive to what others are going through.** We often see the outward appearance of others. But we have no idea what they may really be going through inside. 1 **Corinthians 12**:25-26 ESV / That there may be no division in the body, but that the members may have the same care for one another. If one member suffers, all suffer

together; if one member is honored, all rejoice together.

5. **Educate self on how to not only help yourself but others.** Mental illness is real. I often help others that are going through. One was an individual voicing their feelings of suicide on social media. I reached out allowing them to share their truth requesting to help and call the hotline for them. The whole process took many hours. They had to wait and could have taken their life. But God allowed intercessors to join, with the permission of the individual, in prayer.

Grateful for sensitivity, we often feel what we are going through is bad, but God puts us on assignment and desires us to do his will. When we don't know how to encourage others, we need to educate ourselves. Sometimes it's unnecessary for us to speak. We just need to listen and let them know we are there for them.

The National Suicide Prevention Lifeline is a United States-based suicide prevention network of over 160 crisis centers that provides 24/7 service via a toll-free hotline with the number 1-800-273-8255. It is available to anyone in suicidal crisis or emotional distress. The caller is routed to their nearest crisis center to receive immediate counseling and local mental health referrals. The Lifeline supports people who call for themselves or someone they care about.

6. **Allowing my broken, shattered, and suppressed pieces to heal.**

7. **Embracing my mental health and setting boundaries was imperative-** It's ok to say NO. I know that now. I had to take the time to nurture myself. This is the only way to prevent drain and overwhelm.

8. **Investing in You.** Investing in self-development and professional development helped

me gain the necessary clarity I needed in so many areas of my life.

All the above allowed me to take time with myself and deal with me.

The pandemic was necessary, and I am grateful for the continued healing, cleansing, and restoration that is taking place.

Staying Calm and Centered in Times of Corona Panic

Cheryl Lacey Donovan

As COVID-19 has slowly made its way into major cities and small suburbs across the nation, it's becoming increasingly more difficult to remain calm and not panic.

We have been told by authorities to stay in our homes to prevent spread, but that does not mean that we should go crazy inside and solely focus our attention on what is happening with the world outside. Try to limit how much news you watch, especially some of the overhyped reporting that only propagates fear and anxiety. First and foremost, get updates and facts from reliable sources, and then focus your attention elsewhere.

You can avoid contact with other people and wash your hands more carefully, but your ability to remain calm comes from within. That means you'll have to take the necessary steps in reducing your stress and anxiety and promoting calmness while the virus runs its course.

We're going to go over three of the best ways that you can stay calm and centered in times of COVID-19 panic!

Meditation & Mindfulness

So, you're anxious and stressed as a result of the rapid spread of Coronavirus. If you've never attempted meditation or any mindfulness techniques in the past, this is the perfect time to try them out and get some practice under your belt.

According to the Mayo Clinic, meditation can play a huge role in helping you to maintain your mental and emotional health, even benefiting aspects of your physical health. Here's what meditation can do for you.

- Greater outlook on life (positivity)
- Increased feelings of calmness
- Greater self-awareness
- Reduced levels of anxiety and stress.
- Improved focus

The best part is: There are plenty of different types of meditation.

If you're able to focus for long periods of time, you might want to try out guided meditations or visualization techniques. When you're looking to stay more active while you're quarantined, you can give yoga or Pilates a go!

And for my deep and spiritual sisters and brothers, remember this, "how blessed is the man who does not walk in the counsel of the wicked,

Nor stand in the path of sinners, Nor sit in the seat of scoffers! But his delight is in the law of the LORD, And in His law, he meditates day and night." Psalm 1

Finding a Creative Outlet

You might be stuck in the house for the next few weeks, but that doesn't mean you have to resort to going stir crazy. In fact, that'll probably only increase your feelings of panic during such trying times!

Sheltering in place is a great time to try out some new (or old) creative hobbies. When you're focused on building or creating something new, you're reducing the amount of focus on the negativity surrounding you. That means creativity is a solid way of helping you to relax.

A creative outlet can be almost anything. Here are a few things you might want to try out (if you have the supplies in your home).

- Painting, coloring, or drawing
- Singing or playing musical instruments
- Taking photos or videos of things you enjoy
- Building something with things lying around the house
- Writing
- Puzzles
- Reading something and then writing an essay about it (yes, remember English 101 class?). There couldn't be a better way to take your mind off the world's troubles.

Basically, the goal here is to find an activity or task that requires an intense amount of focus and makes you happy. You won't even notice that you spent the last hour drawing your favorite cartoon character.

Giving Back & Helping Others

When you're giving back to the community or helping those in need, you'll be working to spread compassion and happiness rather than fear and anxiety.

With so many people sick or self-quarantined, most people aren't permitted to leave home. However, these individuals do still have needs that they now can't meet on their own.

If you're keeping your distance and not exposing anyone to the virus, you can deliver food and groceries or do things like their yard work. It'll make you feel good about yourself while also helping those who need it! So, call your neighbors, post something on your Facebook to let those in need know you are available and how to get in contact.

You can't do anything yourself when it comes to curing or stopping the spread of COVID-19, but there are things you can do that can reduce your panic and invoke an overwhelming sense of calmness.

By taking advantage of mindfulness, looking for a creative outlet, and even giving back to those who need it, you'll be able to stay calm and centered, even now!

A Prayerful Response to the Coronavirus

Cheryl Lacey Donovan

"Peace I leave with you; my peace I give you. I do not give to you as the world gives. Do not let your hearts be troubled and do not be afraid." – John 14:27

We're standing in the middle of troubled times. The Coronavirus is a globally spreading pandemic, affecting people from every continent and every walk of life. The young, the old, and everyone in-between are at risk.

It's easy to panic in this place. Maybe you find yourself tempted to hoard supplies, anxiously watching the news, or fretting over all the horrible things that *could* happen to you and your loved ones.

These are natural and normal human reactions to chaotic moments. But just because panic is a tempting reaction doesn't make it your only choice.

There's another option that you may be tempted to overlook—peace.

What Is Peace?

Often, we think of peace as a delightful blessing that we happen to stumble upon every now and again. Maybe you felt peace when you took a day off in the middle of the week to go spend time at the beach or when you heard the news that a loved one's cancer hasn't returned.

But peace isn't just an unexpected blessing.

It's also a choice.

Peace is something we can choose to walk in, even in the middle of the Coronavirus, even in the face of a global pandemic, even when we fear losing our jobs and even when we worry about feeding our families.

How Can We Find Peace in Moments Like These?

It starts with turning your eyes to the throne of God. In Psalm 47:8, the Psalmist proclaimed, "God reigns over the nations; God is seated on his holy throne."

Just as these words were true over 2,000 years ago, they're still true today. God is still on the throne. He still reigns.

Pause to meditate on that truth for just a moment, friend. Despite the chaos, pain, and heartbreak we are encountering in the world today, God maintains absolute control.

Where Is God Right Now?

In Matthew 10:29, Jesus proclaims, "Are not two sparrows sold for a penny? Yet not one of them will fall to the ground outside your Father's care. And even the very hairs of your head are all numbered. So don't be afraid; you are worth more than many sparrows."

You are precious to God. He knit your cells together. He chose the color of your eyes and picked the type of pair you'd have. He painted on your freckles and rejoiced to give you that "birthmark" on your back. He loves your heart and delights in the sound of your laughter.

In the middle of chaos, it's easy to forget these facts. It's tempting to believe that God is distant, but He's never been closer to you. He loves you, and He loves those you love.

Does God Care about the Coronavirus?

Matthew 14:14 reads, "When Jesus landed and saw a large crowd, he had compassion on them and healed their sick."

When Jesus came to earth, one of the marks of His ministry was His healing power over every disease and disability. Some people were cured of an illness by simply touching the hem of His garment.

The same Jesus who had compassion on the sick and frail thousands of years ago still has compassion for those who suffer. He still cares deeply about every sniffle, cold, flu, and virus we encounter on this earth.

What Can I Do to Share My Faith?

If you're a Christian today, you can rejoice. You are standing in the middle of a wonderful opportunity to share your faith. Never have people been more desperate for words of encouragement and hope.

You can sow seeds of love and grace by being kind to those around you (including those you encounter in the grocery store and at the doctor's office).

You can show Christ's love by refusing to hoard supplies or even better, sharing your resources with those who don't have any. You can share God's peace by choosing to remember God's care and provision in times past.

Let's Pray Together…

God, today we rejoice in Your Sovereignty. We choose to remember that You are in control and no virus, flu, or illness can enter our lives without Your Divine permission. You alone hold the power of life and death.

We pray for those who have been affected and will be affected by Coronavirus. We ask for complete healing over their bodies and continual peace over their hearts and minds. We ask for speedy recoveries and a return to full-strength.

We pray for those who are working in the medical profession right now. These healers are certainly close to Your heart. Please, protect them from this awful disease. Comfort them as they comfort others. Encourage them in the middle of the battle and remind them that You are near.

Just as You have full control over every virus, Father, we ask You to stop this one. Hasten the development of vaccines or another cure. Let no more lives be lost to this deadly disease.

Finally, God, we pray for those who have lost or will lose loved ones to the Coronavirus. Walk with these precious souls. Let us be compassionate, quick to grieve with those who are grieving, sharing their sorrows, and comforting them in their affliction.

Thank You for all You've done. Thank You for staying in control, even when the world feels chaotic and scary. Turn our eyes to You in these moments. Keep our gazes fixed on the Cross. In Jesus' name, Amen.